LIFEBOXING

A 90-year life calendar journal for taking control of your days

ANDY LEVENTHLEY

Lifeboxing © Andy Leventhley, 2021
All rights reserved.

No part of this book may be reproduced in any form or by any electronic or mechanical means, including information storage and retrieval systems, without written permission from the author or publisher.

Published by Penhaligon Press

ISBN 978-1-914076-04-6 (paperback)
ISBN 978-1-914076-05-3 (hardback)

How to use your Lifeboxing journal

Welcome to Lifeboxing – a new, productive way to think about your whole life. Many productivity experts recommend the project management method of 'timeboxing' (also known as 'timeblocking') as a way to organize your work or personal life. The idea is that each day is divided into small segments, such as 30 minutes, and you then focus on those one at a time, getting one job done in each time slot. This concept dates back at least to Benjamin Franklin, who allocated time blocks of two or four hours to focus on important or less-important work respectively. Many people today use the Pomodoro technique, breaking the working day down into 25-minute bursts of activity, with five minutes' break in between. In his book *Deep Work*, productivity guru Cal Newport advocates timeblocking, and wrote:

> *"Sometimes people ask why I bother with such a detailed level of planning. My answer is simple: it generates a massive amount of productivity. A 40-hour time-blocked work week, I estimate, produces the same amount of output as a 60+ hour work week pursued without structure."*

Elon Musk and Bill Gates are both known to use this technique, so there must be something going for it!

But what about taking a similar approach to *your whole life*? We already divide our lives into days, governed by cycles of light and darkness, activity and sleep; and by the weeks, months and years of the calendar. We all take stock of our lives, but often lack a clear way of getting the big picture. Enter Lifeboxing.

None of us know how long we're going to live, of course, but most people in the Western world can expect to live into their eighties. If you look at this in days, you can say that people typically live for 30,000 days or so. Putting a number on it focuses the mind: that's the time we have to get the things we want out of life done – well, less, because of course we are all already some way along life's journey.

The blogger Tim Urban – who is known for his great TED talk about procrastination, and in fact has links with Elon Musk, wrote a great blog post on his similar concept of the 'life calendar' back in 2014 – you can read it at https://waitbutwhy.com/2014/05/life-weeks.html. He looked at the different phases of life – school, college, work, retirement – in terms of weeks, shaded on a chart of the 52 x 90 weeks of a typical lifespan. He also studied how many famous scientists, artists and sportspeople achieved many of their great feats in the first third of that life. All of which makes it really important to make the best use of however many boxes of time, of *life*, we have.

Lifeboxing takes a similar approach, but offers the new journal format in this book, which you can keep handy and update whenever you wish; and it breaks your lifespan down into individual days. Think of it as a level up from a daily diary – well you could write something very small in each box, but the point is more to get an overview, to take stock, and to think about what you want. One useful method is shade in the individual boxes – you might use red for work-related goals, or to indicate how long you have spent in your current job, say; or green to break down where you have lived or who you have spend time with. You might want to mark milestones on particular days: important turning points in your past life, but also goals for the future. Set a target: mark it on the day, and then you can see how you can break down the steps from here to there. The possibilities are limitless. Another useful motivation technique is the concept of the streak: you mark off each day when you did whatever it was you want to do – read a book, write a blog post, go for a run, make some time for your family, share something inspiring with your kids. The Lifeboxing journal makes it easy to do that – check the days off, one at a time, and you'll soon have a motivating, visual representation of your achievements.

This journal is simply organized to keep it as flexible as possible for your own needs and ideas. The years 0-15 only have a page each on the assumption your Lifeboxing focus will be adult life, but you can still use those early years to mark down formative stages of your life. For ages 16 to 90 (with apologies to nonagenarians), each year of your life has a two-page spread, with one box for each day, starting with your birthday at the top left – or, if you prefer, of course, you could decide to use each spread for a calendar year. (Note there are 366 day boxes each time, but of course you may want to cross off the extra one where it wasn't or won't be a leap year.)[1] And you can use the four extra boxes at the bottom of each right-hand page to create your own 'key' to symbols/colors you've used in the main boxes. Finally, at the front of the journal is a summary 'Life in a page', where you can step back even further and look at your whole life in one go.

And while looking at the span of life can sometimes be a little daunting, it can also be a source of calm reflection – a stoic acceptance of the passage of time. And remember, as Tim Urban says, "The boxes can also be a reminder that life is forgiving." Each new day brings a fresh new square of opportunity. Good luck with yours, and making Lifeboxing help you get a fresh perspective!

---

[1] Leap years between 1930 and 2100 are: 1932, 1936, 1940, 1944, 1948, 1952, 1956, 1960, 1964, 1968, 1972, 1976, 1980, 1984, 1988, 1992, 1996, 2000, 2004, 2008, 2012, 2016, 2020, 2024, 2028, 2032, 2036, 2040, 2044, 2048, 2052, 2056, 2060, 2064, 2068, 2072, 2076, 2080, 2084, 2088, 2092, 2096 – but not 2100!

A life on a page

0	1	2	3	4	5	6	7	8
9	10	11	12	13	14	15	16
17	18	19	20	21	22	23	24	25
26	27	28	29	30	31	32	33
34	35	36	37	38	39	40	41	42
43	44	45	46	47	48	49	50
51	52	53	54	55	56	57	58	59
60	61	62	63	64	65	66	67
68	69	70	71	72	73	74	75	76
77	78	79	80	81	82	83	84
85	86	87	88	89	90

Age: 0

Age: 1

| 1 | | | | | | | | | | | | | | | |

Age: 2

Age: 3

3

Age: 4

Age: 5

Age: 6

Age: 7

Age: 8

Age: 9

Age: 10

Age: 11

11

Age: 12

Age: 13

13

Age: 14

Age: 15

15

Age: 16

16

Age: 16

Age: 17

17

Age: 17

Age: 18

18

Age: 18

Age: 19

Age: 19

Age: 19

Age: 20

20

Age: 20

Age: 21

|21| | | | | | | | | | | | |

Age: 21

Age: 22

22

Age: 22

Age: 23

23

Age: 23

Age: 24

24

Age: 24

Age: 25

25

Age: 25

Age: 26

26

Age: 26

Age: 27

27

Age: 27

Age: 28

28

Age: 28

Age: 29

29

Age: 29

Age: 30

30												

Age: 30

Age: 30

Age: 31

31

Age: 31

Age: 32

32

Age: 32

Age: 32

Age: 33

33

Age: 33

Age: 34

34

Age: 34

Age: 35

35

Age: 35

Age: 36

36

Age: 36

Age: 37

37

Age: 37

Age: 38

38

Age: 38

Age: 39

39

Age: 39

Age: 40

40

Age: 40

Age: 41

Age: 41

Age: 42

42

Age: 42

Age: 42

Age: 43

43

Age: 43

Age: 44

Age: 44

Age: 45

45

Age: 45

Age: 46

46

Age: 46

Age: 47

47

Age: 47

Age: 48

48

Age: 48

Age: 49

49

Age: 49

Age: 50

50

Age: 50

Age: 51

51

Age: 51

Age: 52

52

Age: 52

Age: 53

53

Age: 53

Age: 54

Age: 54

Age: 55

55

Age: 55

Age: 56

56

Age: 56

Age: 57

57

Age: 57

Age: 58

58

Age: 58

Age: 59

59

Age: 59

Age: 60

60

Age: 60

Age: 61

61

Age: 61

Age: 62

Age: 62

Age: 62

Age: 63

63

Age: 63

Age: 64

64

Age: 64

Age: 65

65

Age: 65

Age: 66

66

Age: 66

Age: 67

67

Age: 67

Age: 68

68

Age: 68

Age: 69

Age: 69

Age: 70

70

Age: 70

Age: 71

71

Age: 71

Age: 72

72

Age: 72

Age: 72

Age: 73

73

Age: 73

Age: 74

74

Age: 74

Age: 75

Age: 75

Age: 76

76

Age: 76

Age: 77

77

Age: 77

Age: 78

78

Age: 78

Age: 79

Age: 79

Age: 80

80

Age: 80

Age: 81

81

Age: 81

Age: 82

Age: 82

Age: 82

Age: 83

83

Age: 83

Age: 84

84

Age: 84

Age: 85

85

Age: 85

Age: 86

86

Age: 86

Age: 87

87

Age: 87

Age: 88

88

Age: 88

Age: 89

89

Age: 89

Age: 90

90

Age: 90

www.ingramcontent.com/pod-product-compliance
Lightning Source LLC
Chambersburg PA
CBHW060506240426
43661CB00007B/937